WILD EARTH
AND OTHER POEMS

THE MACMILLAN COMPANY
NEW YORK · BOSTON · CHICAGO · DALLAS
ATLANTA · SAN FRANCISCO

MACMILLAN & CO., LIMITED
LONDON · BOMBAY · CALCUTTA
MELBOURNE

THE MACMILLAN CO. OF CANADA, LTD.
TORONTO

WILD EARTH

AND OTHER POEMS

BY

PADRAIC COLUM

Author of "Three Plays," "My Irish Year"
"The King of Ireland's Son"

New York
THE MACMILLAN COMPANY
1927

All rights reserved

PRINTED IN THE UNITED STATES OF AMERICA
BY BERWICK & SMITH CO.

CONTENTS

WILD EARTH
AND OTHER POEMS

THE PLOUGHER

Sunset and silence! A man: around him earth savage,
   earth broken;
Beside him two horses—a plough!

Earth savage, earth broken, the brutes, the dawn man
   there in the sunset,
And the Plough that is twin to the Sword, that is founder
   of cities!

" Brute-tamer, plough-maker, earth-breaker! Can'st hear?
   There are ages between us.
" Is it praying you are as you stand there alone in the
   sunset?

" Surely our sky-born gods can be naught to you, earth
   child and earth master?
" Surely your thoughts are of Pan, or of Wotan, or
   Dana?

" Yet, why give thought to the gods? Has Pan led your
   brutes where they stumble?
" Has Dana numbed pain of the child-bed, or Wotan
   put hands to your plough?

" What matter your foolish reply! O, man, standing
 lone and bowed earthward,
" Your task is a day near its close. Give thanks to the
 night-giving God."

.   .   .   .

Slowly the darkness falls, the broken lands blend with
 the savage;
The brute-tamer stands by the brutes, a head's breadth
 only above them.

A head's breadth? Ay, but therein is hell's depth, and
 the height up to heaven,
And the thrones of the gods and their halls, their chariots,
 purples, and splendors.

A DROVER

To Meath of the pastures,
From wet hills by the sea,
Through Leitrim and Longford,
Go my cattle and me.

I hear in the darkness
Their slipping and breathing—
I name them the bye-ways
They're to pass without heeding;

Then the wet, winding roads,
Brown bogs with black water;
And my thoughts on white ships
And the King o' Spain's daughter.

O! farmer, strong farmer!
You can spend at the fair;
But your face you must turn
To your crops and your care.

And soldiers—red soldiers!
You've seen many lands;
But you walk two by two,
And by captain's commands.

5

O! the smell of the beasts,
The wet wind in the morn;
And the proud and hard earth
Never broken for corn;

And the crowds at the fair,
The herds loosened and blind,
Loud words and dark faces
And the wild blood behind.

(O! strong men, with your best
I would strive breast to breast,
I could quiet your herds
With my words, with my words.)

I will bring you, my kine,
Where there's grass to the knee;
But you'll think of scant croppings
Harsh with salt of the sea.

THE FURROW AND THE HEARTH

I

STRIDE the hill, sower,
Up to the sky-ridge,
Flinging the seed,
Scattering, exultant!
Mouthing great rhythms
To the long sea beats
On the wide shore, behind
The ridge of the hillside.

Below in the darkness—
The slumber of mothers—
The cradles at rest—
The fire-seed sleeping
Deep in white ashes!

Give to darkness and sleep:
O sower, O seer!
Give me to the Earth.
With the seed I would enter.
O! the growth thro' the silence
From strength to new strength;
Then the strong bursting forth
Against primal forces,
To laugh in the sunshine,
To gladden the world!

II

Who will bring the red fire
Unto a new hearth?
Who will lay the wide stone
On the waste of the earth?

Who is fain to begin
To build day by day?
To raise up his house
Of the moist, yellow clay?

There's clay for the making
Moist in the pit,
There are horses to trample
The rushes thro' it.

Above where the wild duck
Arise up and fly,
There one may build
To the wind and the sky.

There are boughs in the forest
To pluck young and green,
O'er them thatch of the crop
Shall be heavy and clean.

I speak unto him
Who in dead of the night
Sees the red streaks
In the ash deep and white.

While around him he hears
Men stir in their rest,
And stir of the child
That is close to the breast!

He shall arise,
He shall go forth alone.
Lay stone on the earth
And bring fire to the stone.

WHAT THE SHUILER SAID AS SHE LAY BY
THE FIRE IN THE FARMER'S HOUSE

I'M glad to lie on a sack of leaves
By a wasted fire and take my ease.
For the wind would strip me bare as a tree—
The wind would blow old age upon me.
And I'm dazed with the wind, the rain, and the
        cold.
    If I had only the good red gold
To buy me the comfort of a roof,
And under the thatch the brown of the smoke!
    I'd lie up in my painted room
Until my hired girl would come;
And when the sun had warmed my walls
I'd rise up in my silks and shawls,
And break my fast before the fire.
And I'd watch them that had to sweat
And shiver for shelter and what they ate.
The farmer digging in the fields;
The beggars going from gate to gate;
The horses striving with their loads,
And all the sights upon the roads.

I'd live my lone without clan or care,
And none about me to crave a share.
The young have mocking, impudent ways,
And I'd never let them a-nigh my place.
And a child has often a pitiful face.

I'd give the rambling fiddler rest,
And for me he would play his best.
And he'd have something to tell of me
From the Moat of Granard down to the sea!
And, though I'd keep distant, I'd let in
Old women who would card and spin
And clash with me, and I'd hear it said,
   "Mór who used to carry her head
As if she was a lady bred—
Has little enough in her house, they say—
And such-a-one's child I saw on the way
Scaring crows from a crop, and glad to get,
In a warmer house, the bit to eat.
O! none are safe, and none secure,
And it's well for some whose bit is sure!"

   I'd never grudge them the weight of their lands
If I had only the good red gold
To huggle between my breast and hands!

A CONNACHTMAN

It's my fear that my wake won't be quiet,
  Nor my wake-house a silent place:
For who would keep back the hundreds
  Who would touch my breast and my face?

For the good men were always my friends,
  From Galway back into Clare.
In strength, in sport, and in spending,
  I was foremost at the fair.

In music, in song, and in friendship,
  In contests by night and by day,
By all who knew it was given to me
  That I bore the branch away.

Now let Manus Joyce, my friend
  (If he be at all in the place),
Make smooth the boards of the coffin
  They will put above my face.

The old men will have their stories
  Of all the deeds in my days,
And the young men will stand by the coffin
  And be sure and clear in my praise.

But the girls will stay near the door,
  And they'll have but little to say:
They'll bend their heads, the young girls,
  And for a while they will pray.

And, going home in the dawning,
  They'll be quiet with the boys:
The girls will walk together,
  And seldom they'll lift the voice.

And then, between daybreak and dark,
  And between the hill and the sea,
Three Women, come down from the Mountain,
  Will raise the Keen over me.

But 'tis my grief that I will not hear
  When the cuckoo cries in Glenart,
That the wind that lifts when the sails are loosed
  Will never lift my heart.

AN OLD WOMAN OF THE ROADS

O, to have a little house!
To own the hearth and stool and all!
The heaped up sods upon the fire,
The pile of turf against the wall!

To have a clock with weights and chains
And pendulum swinging up and down!
A dresser filled with shining delph,
Speckled and white and blue and brown!

I could be busy all the day
Clearing and sweeping hearth and floor,
And fixing on their shelf again
My white and blue and speckled store!

I could be quiet there at night
Beside the fire and by myself,
Sure of a bed and loth to leave
The ticking clock and the shining delph!

Och! but I'm weary of mist and dark,
And roads where there's never a house nor bush,
And tired I am of bog and road,
And the crying wind and the lonesome hush!

And I am praying to God on high,
And I am praying Him night and day,
For a little house—a house of my own—
Out of the wind's and the rain's way.

A RANN OF EXILE

Nor right, nor left, nor any road I see a comrade face,
Nor word to lift the heart in me I hear in any place;
They leave me, who pass by me, to my loneliness and care.
Without a house to draw my step nor a fire that I might
    share!

Ocón! before our people knew the scatt'ring of the dearth,
Before they saw potatoes rot and melt black in the earth,
I might have stood in Connacht, on the top of Cruch-
    maelinn,
And all around me I would see the hundreds of my kin.

A RANN OF WANDERING

On Saint Bride's day, when it comes, I will throw a sail
    on the lake,
And in Cahir of my kindred on a fine day I'll awake,
There the hounds will go before us, and make music
    of delight;
And the fires will be piled up there, and the tables spread
    at night;

O, my courage will be mounting up until my spirit's so,
That within a mile of the World's Mouth I will be fain
    to go:
Sure the scatt'ring of the mist across leaves no half wish
    behind,
And my heart was always lifted with the lifting of the
    wind.

THE BEGGAR'S CHILD

MAVOURNEEN, we'll go far away
From the net of the crooked town,
Where they grudge us the light of the day.

Around my neck you will lay
Two tight little arms of brown.
  Mavourneen, we'll go far away
  From the net of the crooked town.

And what will we hear on the way?
The stir of wings up and down, says she,
In nests where the little birds stay!
  Mavourneen, we'll go far away
  From the net of the crooked town,
  Where they grudge us the light of the day.

THE BALLAD OF DOWNAL BAUN
(Domhnal Ban)

The moon-cradle's rocking and rocking,
Where a cloud and a cloud goes by:
Silently rocking and rocking,
The moon-cradle out in the sky.

The hound's in his loop at the fire,
The bond-woman spins at the door;
One rides on a horse through the court-yard:
The sword-sheath drops on the floor.

I

My grandfather, Downal Baun,
Had the dream that comes three times:
He dreamt it first when, a serving boy,
He lay by the nets and the lines,

In the house of Fargal More,
And by Fargal's ash-strewn fire,
When Downal had herded the kine in the waste,
And had foddered them all in the byre;

And he dreamt the dream when he lay
Under sails that were spread to the main;
When he took his rest amid dusky seas,
On the deck of a ship of Spain;

And the dream came to him beneath
The roof he had raised in his pride;
When beside him there lay and dreamt of her kin,
His strange and far-brought bride.

II

He had dreamt three times of the treasure
That fills a broken tale:
The hoard of the men who had raised the mounds,
Who had brewed the Heather Ale;

And he knew by the thrice-come dream
He could win the kist by right,
If he drew it out of the lake by a thread
Upon Saint Bridghid's Night,
By a thread that was bound to the yoke of an ox
That had never a hair of white!

III

So Downal, the silent man,
Went to many a far-off fair,
And he bought him an ox no man could say
Was white by a single hair;

And he came to the edge of the lake
Where no curlew cried overhead:
Silent and bare from the shaking reeds
The lake-waters spread;

And he found it afloat on the current,
The yoke that was hard for the brunt;
And he took the yoke and he bound it,
Across the ox its front;

The yoke had a thread: in the water
He saw the burthened net:
By the push of the ox, by the pull of the thread
Towards the shore the kist was set!

Gold cups for Downal Baun,
Sword-hilts that Kings' hands wore!
O the thread drew the treasure nearer
Till the ripples touched the shore!

Red rings for Downal's bride,
White silver for her rein!
But weight was laid on each mesh of the net,
And the lake held its own again!

He said, " I will break their strength,
Though they put forth all of their might,
For to me was given the yoke and the dream
And the ox with no hair of white."

He whispered, " Labor, O Creature; "
The wide-horned head was set;
The runnels came from eyes, nose and mouth;
The thick hide was all sweat;

Wild Earth

"Forgive me the goad, O Creature!"
It hunched from foreleg to flank,
Heaved; then the yoke on its forehead
Split, and the treasure sank;
And Downal was left with the broken yoke,
And the silent ox on the bank.

He turned the ox to the sedges;
He took it and held the yoke up;
Then he flung it far back in the waters
Of the dark mountain-cup;

And he shouted, "Doomsters, I know
Till five score years from this night,
The treasure is lost, and I trow
My ox has the hair of white."

He stood by the ox its front,
And brute and man were still;
And Downal saw lights burn on the lake,
And fires within the hill.

IV

He turned: a horse was beside him;
It was white as his ox was black;
Who rode it was a woman:
She paced with him down the track;

And along a road not straitened
By ridge or tower or wood,
And past where the Stones of Morna
Like headless giants stood;

And then on the Night of Saint Bridghid
The prayer of her vigil he said
When he looked on the white-horsed woman,
And saw the sign on her head.

" The silks that I wear to my elbows,
The golden clasps at my side,
The silver upon my girdle—
I will give them for your bride."

" Such gear, O Horned Woman,
 Makes due a pledge, I deem."
" Nay. I will gift you freely,
And you shall tell your dream."

" They say that whoever tells not
His dream till he hears the birds—
That man will know the prophecies
In long-remembered words."

" Nay. Tell your dream. Then this hazel
Distaff your wife will gain;"
" The thing that comes in silence," he said,
" In silence must remain."

" O dream-taught man," said the woman—
She stood where the willows grew,
A woman from the country
Where the cocks never crew!

" O dream-taught man," said the woman—
She stayed by a running stream—
" As wise, as wise as the man," she said,
" Who never told his dream."

Then, swift as the flight of the sea-pie,
White woman, white horse, went away;
And Downal passed his haggard,
And faced the spear of the day;

And brought his ox to the byre,
And gave it a measure of straw—
" A white hair you have," said Downal,
" But my plough you are fit to draw,

" And for no dream you'll be burthened,
And for none you will bear the yoke."
Then he lifted the latch of his house-door,
And his bride at his coming awoke;
He drank the milk that she gave him,
And the bread she had made he broke.

The ox was his help thereafter
When he ploughed the upland and lea,
And the growth on the Ridge of the Black Ox
Had a place in men's memory.

And my grandfather, Downal Baun,
Henceforth grew in gains where he stood—
Strong salmon of Lough Oughter,
Gray hawk of the shady wood!

The moon-cradle's rocking and rocking,
Where a cloud and a cloud goes by:
Silently rocking and rocking,
The moon-cradle out in the sky.

To-morrow we'll gather the rushes,
And plait them beside our fire,
And we'll make Saint Bridghid's Crosses,
To hang in the room and the byre.

SHE MOVED THROUGH THE FAIR

My young love said to me, "My brothers won't mind,
And my parents won't slight you for your lack of kind."
Then she stepped away from me, and this she did say,
"It will not be long, love, till our wedding day."

She stepped away from me and she moved through the
    fair,
And fondly I watched her go here and go there,
Then she went her way homeward with one star awake,
As the swan in the evening moves over the lake.

The people were saying no two were e'er wed
But one had a sorrow that never was said,
And I smiled as she passed with her goods and her gear,
And that was the last that I saw of my dear.

I dreamt it last night that my young love came in,
So softly she entered, her feet made no din;
She came close beside me, and this she did say,
"It will not be long, love, till our wedding day."

ACROSS THE DOOR

THE fiddles were playing and playing,
  The couples were out on the floor;
From converse and dancing he drew me,
  And across the door.

Ah! strange were the dim, wide meadows,
  And strange was the cloud-strewn sky,
And strange in the meadows the corncrakes,
  And they making cry!

The hawthorn bloom was by us,
  Around us the breath of the south.
White hawthorn, strange in the night-time—
  His kiss on my mouth!

A CRADLE SONG

O, MEN from the fields!
Come gently within.
Tread softly, softly,
O! men coming in.

Mavourneen is going
From me and from you,
Where Mary will fold him
With mantle of blue!

From reek of the smoke
And cold of the floor,
And the peering of things
Across the half-door.

O, men from the fields!
Soft, softly come thro'.
Mary puts round him
Her mantle of blue.

NO CHILD

I HEARD in the night the pigeons
   Stirring within their nest:
The wild pigeon's stir was tender,
   Like a child's hand at the breast.

I cried, " O, stir no more!
   (My breast was touched of tears),
O pigeons, make no stir—
   A childless woman hears."

INTERIOR

THE little moths are creeping
Across the cottage pane;
On the floor the chickens gather,
And they make talk and complain.

And she sits by the fire
Who has reared so many men;
Her voice is low like the chickens'
With the things she says again.

" The sons that come back do be restless,
They search for the thing to say;
Then they take thought like the swallows,
And the morrow brings them away.

" In the old, old days, upon Innish,
The fields were lucky and bright,
And if you lay down you'd be covered
By the grass of one soft night."

She speaks and the chickens gather,
And they make talk and complain,
While the little moths are creeping
Across the cottage pane.

THREE SPINNING SONGS

I

(A young girl sings:)
THE Lannan Shee
Watched the young man Brian
Cross over the stile towards his father's door,
And she said, "No help,
For now he'll see
His byre, his bawn and his threshing floor!
And oh, the swallows
Forget all wonders
When walls with the nests rise up once more."
  My strand is knit.

"Out of the dream
Of me, into
The round of his labor he will grow;
To spread his fields
In the winds of Spring,
And tramp the heavy glebe and sow;
And cut and clamp
And rear the turf
Until the season when they mow."
  My wheel runs smooth.

" And while he toils
In field and bog
He will be anxious in his mind—
About the thatch
Of barn and rick
Against the reiving autumn wind,
And how to make
His gap and gate
Secure against the thieving kind."
    My wool is fine.

" He has gone back,
And I'll see no more
Mine image in his deepening eyes;
Then I'll lean above
The Well of the Bride,
And with my beauty peace will rise!
O autumn star
In a hidden lake,
Fill up my heart and make me wise!"
    My quick brown wheel!

" The women bring
Their pitchers here
At the time when the stir of the house is o'er;
They'll see my face
In the well-water,
And they'll never lift their vessels more.
For each will say,
' How beautiful—

Why should I labor any more!
Indeed I come
Of a race so fair
'Twere waste to labor any more!'"
      My thread is spun.

II

(An elder girl sings:)
One came before her and said beseeching,
"I have fortune and I have lands,
And if you will share in the goods of my house-
      hold
All my treasure 's at your commands."

But she said to him, "The goods you proffer
Are far from my mind as the silk of the sea!
The arms of him, my young love, round me
Is all the treasure that's true for me!"

" Proud you are then, proud of your beauty,
But beauty's a flower will soon decay;
The fairest flowers they bloom in the Summer,
They bloom one summer and they fade away."

" My heart is sad, then, for the little flower
That must so wither where fair it grew—
He who has my heart in keeping,
I would he had my body too."

III

(An old woman sings:)
There was an oul' trooper went riding by
On the road to Carricknabauna,
And sorrow is better to sing than cry
On the way to Carricknabauna!
And as the oul' trooper went riding on
He heard this sung by a crone, a crone
On the road to Carricknabauna!

" I'd spread my cloak for you, young lad,
Were it only the breadth of a farthen',
And if your mind was as good as your word
In troth, it's you I'd rather!
In dread of any jealousy,
And before we go any farther,
Carry me up to the top of the hill
And show me Carricknabauna! "

" Carricknabauna, Carricknabauna,
Would you show me Carricknabauna?
I lost a horse at Cruckmoylinn—
At the Cross of Bunratty I dropped a limb—
But I left my youth on the crown of the hill
Over by Carricknabauna! "

Girls, young girls, the rush-light is done.
What will I do till my thread is spun?

STORIES

THE Kings of Murias heard that King Atlas had to bear
The World upon his back, so they sent him then and
there
The Crystal Egg that would be the Swan of Endless
Tales
That his burthen for a while might lie on his shoulder-
scales
Fair-balanced, while he heard the Tales the Swan poured
forth—
North-world Tales for the while he watched the Star of
the North;
And East-world Tales he would hear in the morning
swart and cool
When the Lions Nimrod spared came up from the drink-
ing-pool;
West-world Tales would arise when he turned him with
the sun;
Then whispers of Magic Tales from Africa, his own.

But the Kings of Murias made the Crane their mes-
senger—
The fitful Crane whose thoughts are always frightening
her—
She slipped from Islet to Isle, she sloped from foreland
to coast,

She passed through cracks in the mountains, and came
 over trees like a ghost;
And then fled back in dismay when she saw on the hollow
 plains
The final battle between the Pigmies and the Cranes.

Where is the Crystal Egg that was sent King Atlas then?
Hatched it will be one day and the Tales will be told
 to men—
That is if the fitful Crane did not lose it threading the
 Sea;
That is if it is not laid in some King's old Treasury!

THE TERRIBLE ROBBER MEN

O! I wish the sun was bright in the sky,
  And the fox was back in his den, O!
For always I'm hearing the passing by
  Of the terrible robber men, O!
    The terrible robber men.

O! what does the fox carry over the rye
  When it's bright in the morn again, O!
And what is it making the lonesome cry
  With the terrible robber men, O!
    The terrible robber men.

O! I wish the sun was bright in the sky,
  And the fox was back in his den, O!
For always I'm hearing the passing by
  Of the terrible robber men, O!
    The terrible robber men.

AN DRINAUN DONN

(From the Irish)

A hundred men think I am theirs when with them I
    drink ale,
But their presence fades away from me, and their high
    spirits fail,
When I think upon your converse kind by the meadow
    and the linn,
And your form smoother than the silk on the Mountain
    of O'Flynn.

Oh, Paddy, is it pain to you that I'm wasting night and
    day,
And, Paddy, is it grief to you that I'll soon be in the clay?
My first love with the winning mouth, my treasure you'll
    abide,
Till the narrow coffin closes me, and the grass grows
    through my side.

The man who strains to leap the wall, we think him
    foolish still
When to his hand is the easy ditch to vault across at will:
The rowan tree is fine and high, but bitter its berries
    grow,
While blackberries and raspberries are on shrubs that
    blossom low.

Farewell, farewell, forever, to yon town amongst the
    trees,
Farewell, the town that draws me, on mornings and
    on eves,
Oh, many's the ugly morass now, and many's the crooked
    road,
That lie henceforth between me and where my heart's
    bestowed.

And Mary, Ever Virgin, where will I turn my head!
I know not where his house is built, nor where his fields
    are spread.
Ah, kindly was the counsel that my kinsfolk gave to me,
" The hundred twists are in his heart, and the thousand
    tricks has he."

POLONIUS AND THE BALLAD SINGERS

A GAUNT-BUILT woman and her son-in-law,
A broad-faced fellow, with such flesh as shows
Nothing but easy nature, and his wife,
The woman's daughter, who spills all her talk
Out of a wide mouth, but who has eyes as gray
As Connemara, where the mountain-ash
Shows berries red indeed.—They enter now—
Our country singers!

Sing, my good woman, sing us some romance
That has been round your chimney-nooks so long
'Tis nearly native—something blown here
And since made racy—like yon tree, I might say—
Native by influence if not by species—
Shaped by our winds—You understand, I think?

—I'll sing the song, sir—

To-night you see my face—
Maybe never more you'll gaze
On the one that for you left his friends and kin;
For by the hard commands
Of the lord that rules these lands
On a ship I'll be borne from Cruckaunfinn!

40

O you know your beauty bright
Has made him think delight
More than from any fair one he will gain;
O you know that all his will
Strains and strives around you till
As the hawk upon his hand you are as tame!

Then she to him replied:
" I'll no longer you deny,
And I'll let you have the pleasure of my charms,
For to-night I'll be your bride,
And whatever may betide
It's we will lie in one another's arms! "

You should not sing
With body doubled up and face aside—
There is a climax here—" It's we will lie—"
Hem—passionate!—And what does your daughter
sing?

—A song I like when I do climb bare hills—
'Tis all about a hawk,—

No bird that sits on rock or bough
Has such a front as thine;
No King that has made war his trade
Such conquest in his eyne!
I know thee rock-like on the rock
Where none can mark a shape;
I climb, but thou dost climb with wings,
And like a wish escape,
She said,
And like a wish escape!

No maid that kissed his bonny mouth
Of another mouth was glad;
Such pride was in our Chieftain's eyes
Such countenance he had!
But since they made him fly the rocks,
Thou, Creature, art my quest,—
Then lift me with thy steady eyes,
If then to tear my breast,
                    She said,
If then to tear my breast!

                    The songs they have
Are the last relics of the feudal world!
Women will keep them—byzants, doubloons,
When men will take up songs that are as new
As dollar-bills.   What song have you, young man?

—A song my father had, sir.   It was sent him
From across the sea, and there was a letter with it,
Asking my father to put it to a tune
And sing it all roads.   He did that, in troth,
And five pounds of tobacco were sent with the song
To forereward him.   I'll sing it for you now—
   " The Baltimore Exile. "

The house I was bred in—ah, does it remain?
Low walls and loose thatch standing lone in the rain,
With the clay of the walls coming through with its stain,
Like the blackbird's left nest in the briar!

Does a child there give heed to the song of the lark,
As it lifts and it drops till the fall of the dark,
When the heavy-foot kine trudge home from the park,
Or do none but the red-shank now listen?

The sloe-bush, I know, grows close to the well,
And its long-lasting blossoms are there I can tell,
When the kid that was yeaned when the first ones befell
Can jump to the ditch that they grow on!

But there's silence on all. Then do none ever pass
On the way to the fair or the pattern or mass?
Do the grey-coated lads drive the ball through the grass
And speed to the sweep of the hurl?

O youths of my Land! Then will no Bolivar
Ever muster your ranks for delivering war?
Will your hopes become fixed and beam like a star?
Will they pass like the mists from your fields?

The swan and the swallow, the cuckoo and crake
May visit my land and find hillside and lake,
And I send my song—I'll not see her awake;
I'm a bird too old to uncage now!

A little silver in a little purse!
Take it and spend it on your journey, Friends.

We will. And may we meet your Honor's like
Every day's end!

A song is more lasting than the voice of the birds!

A word is more lasting than the riches of the world!

THE SEA BIRD TO THE WAVE

On and on,
O white brother!
Thunder does not daunt thee!
How thou movest!
By thine impulse—
With no wing!
Fairest thing
The wide sea shows me!
On and on,
O white brother!

Art thou gone?

THE WAYFARER

I

The Trees

THERE is no glory of the sunset here!
Heavy the clouds upon the darkening road,
And heavy too the wind upon the trees!
The trees sway, making moan
Continuous, like breaking seas.
O impotent, bare things,
You give at last the very cry of Earth!
I walk this darkening road in solemn mood:
Within deep hell came Dante to a wood—
Like him I marvel at the crying trees!

II

Christ the Comrade

Christ, by thine own darkened hour,
Live within me, heart and brain—
Let my hands not slip the rein!

Ah, how long ago it is
Since a comrade went with me!
Now a moment let me see

Thyself, lonely in the dark,
Perfect, without wound or mark!

III

The Captive Archer

To-morrow I will bend the bow:
My soul shall have her mark again,
My bosom feel the archer's strain.
No longer pacing to and fro
With idle hands and listless brain:
As goes the arrow, forth I go.
My soul shall have her mark again,
My bosom feel the archer's strain.
To-morrow I will bend the bow.

IV

Triumphators

The drivers in the sunset race
Their coal-carts over cobble-stones—
Not draymen but triumphators:
Their bags are left with Smith and Jones,
They let their horses take their stride,
Which toss their forelocks in their pride.

Nor blue nor green these factions wear
Which make career o'er Dublin stones;
But Pluto his own livery
Is what each whip-carrier owns.
The Cæsar of the cab-rank, I
Salute the triumph speeding by.

GARADH

For the poor body that I own
    I could weep many a tear:
The hours have stolen flesh and bone,
    And left a changeling here.

Four feeble bones are left to me,
    And the basket of my breast.
And I am mean and ugly now
    As the scald flung from the nest.

The briars drag me at the knee,
    The brambles go within,
And often do I feel him turn
    The old man in my skin.

The strength is carded from my bones,
    The swiftness drained from me.
And all the living thoughts I had
    Are like far ships at sea!

"I SHALL NOT DIE FOR THEE"

(*From the Irish*)

O woman, shapely as the swan,
On your account I shall not die:
The men you've slain—a trivial clan—
Were less than I.

I ask me shall I die for these—
For blossom-teeth and scarlet lips?
And shall that delicate swan shape
Bring me eclipse?

Well-shaped the breasts and smooth the skin,
The cheeks are fair, the tresses free—
And yet I shall not suffer death—
God over me!

Those even brows, that hair like gold,
Those languorous tones, that virgin way—
The flowing limbs, the rounded heel
Slight men betray!

Thy spirit keen through radiant mien,
Thy shining throat and smiling eye,
Thy little palm, thy side like foam—
I cannot die!

O woman, shapely as the swan,
In a cunning house hard-reared was I:
O bosom white, O well-shaped palm,
I shall not die!

OLD MEN COMPLAINING

FIRST OLD MAN:
He threw his crutched stick down: there came
Into his face the anger flame,
And he spoke viciously of one
Who thwarted him—his son's son.
He turned his head away. " I hate
Absurdity of language, prate
From growing fellows. We'd not stay
About the house the whole of a day
      When we were young,
Keeping no job and giving tongue!

" Not us in troth! We would not come
For bit or sup, but stay from home
If we gave answers, or we'd creep
Back to the house, and in we'd peep
Just like a corncrake.

" My grandson and his comrades take
A piece of coal from you, from me
A log, or sod of turf, maybe.
And in some empty place they'll light
A fire, and stay there all night,
A wisp of lads! Now understand
The blades of grass under my hand
Would be destroyed by company!

There's no good company! We go
With what is lowest to the low!
He stays up late, and how can he
Rise early? Sure he lags in bed
And she is worn to a thread
With calling him—his grandmother—
She's an old woman, and she must make
Stir when the birds are half awake
In dread he'd lose this job like the other!"

SECOND OLD MAN:
" They brought yon fellow over here,
And set him up for an overseer:
Though men from work are turned away,
That thick-necked fellow draws full pay,
Three pounds a week. . . . They let burn down
The timber yard behind the town
Where work was good, though firemen stand
In boots and brasses big and grand
The crow of a cock away from the place;
And with the yard they let burn too
The clock in the tower, the clock I knew
As well as I know the look of my face."

THIRD OLD MAN:
" The fellow you spoke of has broken his
    bounds—
He comes to skulk inside of these grounds:
Behind the bushes he lay down
And stretched full hours in the sun.
He rises now, and like a crane

Fine color had my darling though it was not me was
    there:
I did not sit beside her, but inside there was a pair!
I stood outside the window like a poor neglected soul,
And I waited till my own name was brought across the
    coal!

Here's a health unto the blackbird that sings upon the
    tree,
And here's to the willy-wagtail that goes the road with
    me!
Here's a health unto my darling and to them she makes
    her own :
She's deserving of good company; for me, I go my lone.

My love she is courteous and handsome and tall;
For wit and for behavior she's foremost of them all!
She says she is in no ways bound, that with me she'll go
    free;
But my love had too many lovers to have any love for me!

1st Girl

Mallo lero iss im bo nero!
Who weds him might cry with the wandering
    plover!
Mallo lero iss im bo baun!

Mallo lero iss im bo nero!
Where they're breaking the horses, go find me
    my lover!
Mallo lero iss im bo baun!

2nd Girl

Mallo lero iss im bo nero!
Him with the strong hand I will bring from the
    clover.
Mallo lero iss im bo baun!

1st Girl

Mallo lero iss im bo nero!
I wait till I hear what he's singing over.
Mallo lero iss im bo baun!

Another man's voice:

Are they not the good men of Eirinn,
Who give not their thought nor their voice
To fortune, but take without dowry
The maids of their choice?

For the trout has sport in the river,
Whether prices be up or low-down,
And the salmon, he slips through the water,
Not heeding the town!

Then if she, the love of my bosom,
Did laugh as she stood by my door,
O I'd rise then and draw her in to me,
With kisses *go leor!*

It's not likely the wind in the tree-tops
Would trouble my love nor my rest,
Nor the hurrying footsteps would draw her,
My love from my breast!

1st Girl

Mallo lero iss im bo nero!
He sings to the *girsha* in the hazel-wood cover.
Mallo lero iss im bo baun!

Mallo lero iss im bo nero!
Go where they're shearing and find me my lover.
Mallo lero iss im bo baun!

2nd Girl

Mallo lero iss im bo nero!
The newly-come youth is looking straight over!
Mallo lero iss im bo baun!

1st Girl

Mallo lero iss im bo nero!
Mind what he sings, and I'll give you trover!
Mallo lero iss im bo baun!

A young man's voice sings:

Once I went over the Ocean,
On a ship that was bound for proud Spain:
Some people were singing and dancing,
But I had a heart full of pain.

I'll put now a sail on the lake
That's between my treasure and me,
And I'll sail over the lake
Till I come to the Joyce Country.

She'll hear my boat on the shingles,
And she'll hear my step on the land,
And the corncrake hid in the meadow
Will tell her that I'm at hand!

The Summer comes to Glen Nefin
With heavy dew on the leas,
With the gathering of wild honey
To the tops of all the trees;

In honey and dew the Summer
Upon the ground is shed,
And the cuckoo cries until dark
Where my *storeen* has her bed!

And if O'Hanlon's daughter
Will give me a welcome kind,
O never will my sail be turned
To a harsh and a heavy wind!

1st Girl

Mallo lero iss im bo nero!
Welcome I'll give him over and over.
Mallo lero iss im bo baun!

2nd Girl

Mallo lero iss im bo nero!
Go where they're threshing and find me my
lover.
Mallo lero iss im bo baun!

DERMOTT DONN MacMORNA

ONE day you'll come to my husband's door,
    Dermott Donn MacMorna,
One day you'll come to Hugh's dark door,
And the pain at my heart will be no more,
    Dermott Donn MacMorna!

From his bed, from his fire, I'll rise,
    Dermott Donn MacMorna,
From the bed of Hugh, from his fire I'll rise,
With my laugh for the pious, the quiet, the wise,
    Dermott Donn MacMorna!

Lonesome, lonesome, the house of Hugh,
    Dermott Donn MacMorna,
No cradle rocks in the house of Hugh;
The list'ning fire has thought of you,
    Dermott Donn MacMorna!

Out of this loneliness we will go,
    Dermott Donn MacMorna,
Together at last, we two will go
Down a darkening road with a gleam below.
Ah, but the winds do bitter blow,
    Dermott Donn MacMorna!

A POOR SCHOLAR OF THE FORTIES

My eyelids red and heavy are,
With bending o'er the smold'ring peat.
I know the Æneid now by heart,
My Virgil read in cold and heat,
In loneliness and hunger smart.
    And I know Homer, too, I ween,
    As Munster poets know Ossian.

And I must walk this road that winds
'Twixt bog and bog, while east there lies
A city with its men and books,
With treasures open to the wise,
Heart-words from equals, comrade-looks;
    Down here they have but tale and song,
    They talk Repeal the whole night long.

"You teach Greek verbs and Latin nouns,"
The dreamer of Young Ireland said.
"You do not hear the muffled call,
The sword being forged, the far-off tread
Of hosts to meet as Gael and Gall—
    What good to us your wisdom store,
    Your Latin verse, your Grecian lore?"

And what to me is Gael or Gall?
Less than the Latin or the Greek.—
I teach these by the dim rush-light,
In smoky cabins night and week.
But what avail my teaching slight?
    Years hence, in rustic speech, a phrase,
    As in wild earth a Grecian vase!

A BALLAD MAKER

ONCE I loved a maiden fair,
Over the hills and far away,
Lands she had and lovers to spare,
Over the hills and far away.
And I was stooped and troubled sore,
And my face was pale, and the coat I wore
Was thin as my supper the night before.
Over the hills and far away.

Once I passed in the autumn late,
Over the hills and far away,
Her bawn and byre and painted gate,
Over the hills and far away.
She was leaning there in the twilight space,
Sweet sorrow was on her fair young face,
And her wistful eyes were away from the place—
Over the hills and far away.

Maybe she thought as she watched me come,
Over the hills and far away,
With my awkward stride, and my face so glum,
Over the hills and far away,
" Spite of his stoop, he still is young;
They say he goes the Shee among,
Ballads he makes, I've heard them sung
Over the hills and far away."

61

She gave me good-night in gentle wise,
    Over the hills and far away,
Shyly lifting to mine, dark eyes,
    Over the hills and far away.
What could I do but stop and speak,
And she no longer proud but meek?
She plucked me a rose like her wild rose cheek—
    Over the hills and far away.

To-morrow, Mavourneen a sleeveen weds,
    Over the hills and far away,
With corn in haggard and cattle in sheds,
    Over the hills and far away.
And I who have lost her—the dear, the rare—
Well, I got me this ballad to sing at the fair,
'Twill bring enough money to drown my care,
    Over the hills and far away.

AN IDYLL

You stay for a while beside me
With your beauty young and rare,
Though your light limbs are as limber, maid,
As the foal's that follows the mare.
Brow fair and young and stately
Where buds of thought have begun;
Hair bright as the breast of the eagle, maid,
When it strains up to the sun!

In the space of a broken castle
I found you upon a day,
When the call of the new-come cuckoo, maid,
Went with me all the way.
You stood by unmortised stones—
By stones rough and black with age,
The fawn beloved of the hunter, maid,
In the panther's broken cage.

And we went down together
By paths your childhood knew,
Remote you went beside me, maid,
Like the spirit of the dew:
They were hard—the hedgerows—still,
Sloe-bloom was their scanty dower,
You slipped it within your bosom, maid,
The bloom that scarce is flower;

And now you stay beside me,
With your beauty young and rare,
Though your light limbs are as limber, maid,
As the foal's that follows the mare.
Brow fair and young and stately
Where buds of thought have begun,
Hair bright as the breast of the eagle, maid,
When it strains up to the sun.

ARAB SONGS

I. UMIMAH

SAADI, the Poet, stood up and he put forth his living
  words;
His songs were the hurtling of spears, and his figures the
  flashing of swords!
With hearts dilated the tribe saw the creature of Saadi's
  mind:
It was like to the horse of a King—a creature of fire and
  of wind!

Umimah, my loved one, was by me; without love did
  these eyes see my fawn,
And if fire there were in her being for me its splendor
  was gone;
When the sun storms up on the tent it makes waste the
  fire of the grass:
It was thus with my loved one's beauty—the splendor of
  song made it pass!

The desert, the march, and the onset—these, and these
  only avail;
Hands hard with the handling of spear-shafts, brows
  white with the press of the mail!
And as for the kisses of women—these are honey, the
  poet sings,
But the honey of kisses, beloved—it is lime for the
  spirit's wings!

II. The Gadfly

Ye know not why God hath joined the horse-fly unto the
horse,
Nor why the generous steed should be yoked with the
poisonous fly:
Lest the steed should sink into ease and lose his fervor
of limb
God hath bestowed on him this—a lustful and venomous
bride!

Never supine lie they, the steeds of our folk, to the sting,
Praying for deadness of nerve with wounds the shame
of the sun:
They strive, but they strive for this—the fullness of
passionate nerve;
They pant, but they pant for this—the speed that out-
strips the pain!

Sons of the Dust, ye have stung—there is darkness upon
my soul!
Sons of the Dust, ye have stung—yea, stung to the roots
of my heart!
But I have said in my breast—the birth succeeds to the
pang,
And Sons of the Dust, behold—your malice becomes my
song!

III. The Parrot and the Falcon

My Afghan poet-friend
With this made his message end—
" The scroll around my wall shows two the poets have
   known—
      The parrot and falcon they—
      The parrot hangs on his spray,
And silent the falcon sits with brooding and baleful eyes.

   " Men come to me; one says,
      ' We have given your verses praise,
And we will keep your name abreast of the newer names;
      But you must make what accords
      With poems that are household words—
Your own: write familiar things; to your hundred add a
   score.'

   " My friend, they would bestow
      Fame for a shadow-show,
And they would pay with praise for things dead as last
   year's leaves.
      But I look where the parrot, stilled,
      Hangs a head with rumors filled,
And I watch where my falcon turns her brooding and
   baleful eyes!

   " Come to my shoulder! Sit!
   To the bone be your talons knit!

I have sworn my friends shall have no parrot-speech
    for me.
           Who reads the verse I write
           Shall know the falcon's flight,
The vision single and sure, the conquest of air and sun!

Is there aught else worthy to weave within your banners'
    folds?
Is there aught else worthy to grave on the blades of
    your naked swords?"

RIVER MATES

I'LL be an otter, and I'll let you swim
A mate beside me; we will venture down
A deep, full river when the sky above
Is shut of the sun; spoilers are we:—
Thick-coated: no dog's tooth can bite at our veins,
With ears and eyes of poachers: deep-earthed ones
Turned hunters; let him strike past,—
The little vole; my teeth are on an edge
For the King-Fish of the River!
       I hold him up,
The glittering salmon that smells of the sea:
I hold him up and whistle!
       Now we go
Back to our earth: we will tear and eat
Sea-smelling salmon: you will tell the cubs
I am the Booty-bringer—I am the Lord
Of the River—the deep, dark, full and flowing River.

FOR MORFYDD

IT would not be far for us two to go back to the age of
    bronze:
Then you were a King's daughter; your father had cur-
    raghs a score;
A herd of horses, good tillage upon the face of four hills,
And clumps of cattle beyond them where rough-browed
    men showed their spears.

And I was good at the bow, but I had no men and no
    herds,
And your father would have bestowed you, in a while,
    on some unrenowned
Ulysses; or on the high King to whom they afterwards
    raised
Three stones as high as the elk's head (this cromlech,
    maybe, where we sit).

How fair you were when you walked beside the old forest
    trees!
So fair that I thought you would change and fly away
    as a swan!
And then we were mates for play; and then all eagle
    you grew
To drive me to range the tempest—King's child of the
    hero-age!

I called three times as an owl: through the gap where
    the herdsmen watched
You ran, and we climbed the height where the brackens
    pushed at our knees;
And we lay where the brackens drew the earth-smell out
    of the earth,
And we journeyed and baffled the fighters of three ill-
    wishing Kings!

It would not be far for us two to go back to the age of
    bronze—
The fire left by the nomads is lone as a burning ship!
We eat them as we pass by, the sweet green ears of the
    wheat!
At last, a King, I relieve a good clan from a dragon's
    spleen!

Pieces of amber I brought you, big as a bowman's
    thumbs;
Trumpets I left beside you, wrought when the smiths
    had all art;
A dancing-bird that I caught you—they are back in the
    age of bronze:
I give what I made, and found, and caught—a score of
    songs!